AGE IS ONLY A NUMBER

If you read *Age Is Only A Number*
You will see,
I refuse to let age
Get the better of me.

Marcia Bass Brody

AGE IS
ONLY A
NUMBER

POEMS

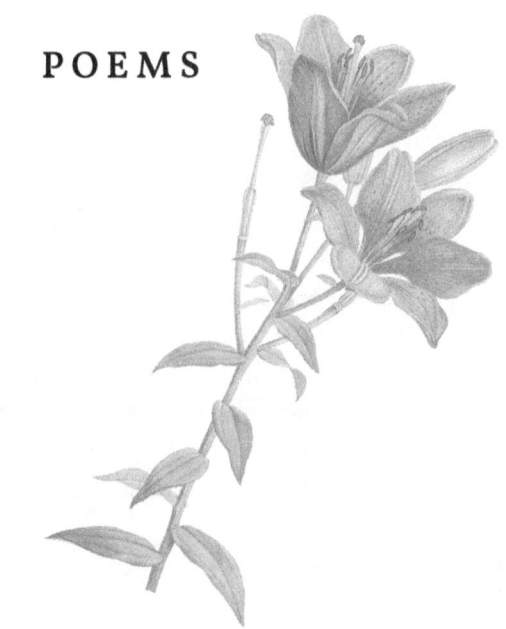

Copyright © 2022, 2024 Marcia Bass Brody
All rights reserved

No part of this book may be used or reproduced in any manner whatsoever without written permission, except in the case of brief quotations embodied in critical articles and reviews.

Production Supervisor: Susan Sonenthal

ISBN: 979-8-8690-4760-1 (paperback)
       978-1-0880-3146-9 (e-book)

Mr. Gray

I met Mr. Gray in my 60's
When I was young and gay
I did not like what I saw so
I sent Mr. Gray away.
Now that I'm in my 90's,
I'm as free as I can be,
I told Mr. Gray to return
And stay forever with me because
My hair loves you.

Visit

If you ever come see me,
You don't have to look far,
I live in the house,
The house without a car.
My neighbors have cars
In driveways and the street,
I seem to get around
On my reliable two feet.
When you decide to visit,
Bring cookies and a treat,
We'll enjoy each others company
While we sit, laugh and eat.

Dates with Professionals

When I was young and had a date,
I'd get dressed up and could not wait.
If he were a professional I would see
All my friends would be jealous of me.
I'm now in my 90's, my hair is grey,
My friends have died and every day
I have dates with professionals
Teeth, Feet, Eyes,
No one is jealous,
Are you surprised?

Itch

Itch, Itch, Itch,
Scratch, scratch, scratch,
That is what happens when your skin
    gets old.
Itch, Itch, Itch,
Scratch, scratch, scratch,
This can happen in weather hot or cold.
My son is now scratching
On lottery tickets he bought today.
I hope his scratching continues
And mine will go away.

Stay Awake

Don't fall asleep
On the toilet seat
When you wake up at two.
Don't fall asleep
On the toilet seat
You can end up black and blue.
A fall is bad,
And it's sad,
If it happens in the middle of the night,
So don't fall asleep on the toilet seat
And you will be alright.

Family

We were seven siblings,
Growing up in North, SC.
Bernie, Herbie, Ruth, Frances are gone,
That leaves Lucille, Jack and me.
In 2022 I hope to be alive
So I can celebrate
When I reach 95.

Family

Are you a father, mother, sister, brother,
　　daughter, son?
Are you a nephew, niece, uncle, aunt,
　　cousin or none?
Always be the best of who you are and
Be glad to be you.

Family

Two in a double bed,
Four girls in a room,
That's how we grew up
in North.
One dresser in the room,
We each had a drawer,
That's how we grew up
in North.
One closet for our clothes
In the 30's,
Pleasant memories and friends
Down south in North.

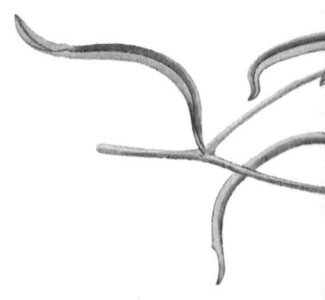

Family

I was speaking to my nephew
Who is now the Honorable Neil,
He is the new City Councilman
Traveling in his automobile.
I remember Neil as a child
Growing up in my sister's fold,
Neil remembers me as middle aged,
Now he considers me old.

Stay in Shape

I cut my nails with a scissors,
I let my hair go gray,
I wake up with aches and pains
When I move it goes away.
I exercise by walking
To the store or around the block,
I do not want my body
To get solid like a rock.

Lifetime

I look in the mirror and what do I see,
A little old lady staring at me.
No facial makeup,
Her hair is all grey,
I wonder if she will return
Another day.

Too Old to Be Fixed

My microwave just broke,
My printer doesn't print,
Everything is starting to go because of age.
My eyesight has decreased, I tire easily,
Everything is starting to go because of age.
I can buy a new microwave,
A printer I can replace,
As for my body, I'll make do with what
    I face,
I still can walk and I make sense when
    I talk,
I refuse to let age take the better of me.

Old Age

We all think it won't happen to me.
Wait until the 90's and you will see
Old is when you go upstairs and then
    go downstairs to remember why
    you went upstairs.
Old is when you repeat what you already
    said.
Old is when you stretch your arms to touch
    your toes and all you can touch are
    your knees.
Old is when your mind wanders and you
    can't remember yesterday.
Old is when your niece asks if you prepaid
    your funeral.
OLD IS REALLY HAVING LIVED A
    LONG TIME.
You can remain young by walking, talking,
    reconnect with people and nature.
Make the most of what you have, think
    positive and enjoy your old age.

Life

I'm at the do it the easy way
In all that I do every day,
Bathing, eating, groceries, socializing,
It can't be complicated in any way.
I have a chair in the shower
I use every day.
When you are in your 90's
You bathe the easy way.
I eat my dinner from a box,
All I have to do is heat,
No peeling, cutting or cooking,
I can relax when I eat.
I talk to few family and friends,
Most of them are dead,
I think I'll go eat dinner,
Then I'll go to bed.
If anyone wants to take me for a ride or
    walk with me, I'm ready!

A Day in the Life of an Elderly Living at Home

I like a navel orange for breakfast
Plus instant oatmeal,
That takes care of me until lunch.
Now that's a good deal.
I can now wash dishes,
Make up my bed,
Throw out papers even though they
 aren't read.
I have bills to pay
Scattered everywhere,
They need to be sorted
Before becoming a nightmare.
Then it's naptime for little old me,
I close the door, turn off the phone and
Sleep sound free.
When I awake, I go for a walk,
If I see a neighbor, I stop and talk.
Dinner is next and what do I eat,
A boxed meal waiting for the heat.
I Need A Vacation!

Age

My towels and sheets
Are getting paper thin,
Everything is starting to go because of age.
My house needs repairs,
My body has slowed down,
Everything is starting to go because of age.
You can try to look young but you can't hide it,
You are asked age for important events
    in life.
For a license when you drive,
For your tombstone when you die,
Everyone wants to know your age.

Age

What's good about the 90's,
When you find out let me know.
Age has affected me,
It has depleted all my dough.
My hair became thin
My body is thick,
I'm tired all the time,
So, what's good about the 90's
When you find out let me know.

Age

I buy my clothes from thrift shops,
My hair gets washed by me,
My funds for food are limited,
When I go to the store at three.
I'm past the age of 94
I'm glad to be alive,
I'm still planning a party
When I reach 95.

Party

I made a promise to myself
When I reached 85,
That I'd give myself a party
Every five years while alive.
In 2022 I'll be 95,
My close friends are gone but
I'm glad to be alive.
I shall be planning that party!!!

Party

When I read the obits,
The first thing I see,
Most who are gone
Were younger than me.
I gave myself a party,
At ages 85 and 90 years,
If I'm still here at 95,
You are invited to come cheer.
August 22, 2022 is the date.

Party

My children have written me off,
They are ready to say I'm no more,
I can still get around
Even though I'm 94.
I can exercise my body
By walking around the block,
I can manage a household,
Though expenses are quite a shock.
Living is hard but I'm glad to be alive and
I still intend to have a party
When I reach 95.

I used to walk our dog,
Now my children walk me out the door,
That's what happens at age 94.
I have to exercise my body and stay alive,
So I can have that party at age 95.

Visit

I've been waiting for your visit since 1985,
You told me to prepare while I'm still alive.
How to react when I open the door,
Have the same reaction if I'm coming from
    the store.
36 years have gone by and I'm still waiting,
For the knock on the door I'm anticipating.
I hope you come while I'm still alive,
So YOU can pay for a party when I
    reach 95.
How much longer, Publishers Clearing
    House?

Lines

There are lines at the grocery store,
There are lines at the mall,
The lines on my face
Are the longest of all.
As people purchase
Lines decrease at the mall, but
The lines on my face remain
In the summer, winter and fall.

Words I Try to Live By

Say little and do much
Can't never could do anything
If you can't say something good about
    someone then don't say anything
Learn to forgive
Look for the good in everyone even though
    in some it's hard to find
Think positive
Remember what others do for you and
    forget what you do for others
Do not live on "ifs" and "should've dones"
First do what you have to do and then do
    what you want to do
When you have something to do, push
    aside the words "later" or "tomorrow"
    and remember the word "now."

Leave a Message

Leave a message when you call,
I might be in the bathroom or the hall,
I could be outside to get the paper
    to be read,
I'm not with my friends because they are
    all dead so
Please leave a message when you call.

Mummy

She is not my mummy as you can see,
Her skin is old and withered as can be.
She cannot hear or see or talk,
She cannot move or go for a walk.
I can think and I can walk,
I still make sense when I talk.
My skin is aging and getting wrinkled
    as can be
But she is still a mummy and I am still me.

Mystery of the Sock

I removed my clothes from the dryer,
They are now nice and clean,
I'm confronted with a problem,
A sock vanished in the machine.
Every sock must have a mate
When you decide to take a walk,
How can you disappear, sock?
If only you could talk.

Confusion in an Elder

I awake all dressed with confusion
    in my brain,
I don't know if it's morning or night,
I look out the window, I'm not in pain.
The sky just doesn't look right.
I still don't know if it's morning or night,
I have to wait and see.
If the sun comes up it's morning and
If the stars come out it's night,
I have to decide how to dress so
I can look alright.

Walker and Cane

There is a walker in my bedroom,
A cane hanging from my door,
I never want to see a hospital
or a rehab anymore.
I want to remain independent,
As long as I can be,
I do not want anyone taking advantage
Of little old me.
I was raised to be honest,
In all that I do,
Most people think of themselves
Before they think of you, so please
Do not take advantage of me.

Don't Stop Reading

I try to have a scissors and pen,
When reading newspapers and opening
    the mail,
There might be a contest to enter,
There may be the date of a sale.
An interesting article may appear,
Which I'll cut out while in my den,
Life becomes interesting because
I have my newspaper, scissors and pen.

Thickness in My Skin—
Not in My Head

I have to call my podiatrist
When I wake up in the morn,
My right foot hurts when I walk,
I have a callus and a corn.
If you are young, you won't understand
That the corn is on my feet,
You can't put it in your mouth,
It is not something to eat.

Age 94

My pants used to reach my ankles,
Now they are covering the floor,
I used to be 5'1" but
I seem to be shrinking more and more.
Everything seems to decrease,
As the many years go by,
Your income, your height,
Your health and your sight
But never your appetite.

Relish Life

Save money for a birthday,
So you can celebrate
A joyful occasion,
Go to a restaurant that's first rate.
Life is full of challenges,
Illness, death and fate,
Enjoy all happy events,
When you die it will be too late.

A New Day

I wake up in the morning
With a pain in my left hip,
I have to move around or
I'll sink like a ship.
I shower, dress, eat breakfast,
That's how I start a new day,
Wash my dish, make my bed,
Then I'm on my way.
I face household clutter,
Papers and bills
A house that needs deep cleaning,
So distressing I need pills (I really mean ice cream)!

Milk with Breakfast

When I was a little girl,
My mother made my meals.
She gave me milk with my breakfast,
That was a big deal.
I immediately said, "Mama,
Please take the chill off my milk.
I do not like milk cold,
I do not like milk hot so
Please take the chill off my milk."
My mother could do anything and
    everything.
She could even take the chill off my milk.

The 96 Club

Would you like to join the 96 Club?
It comes with aches and pain each day
You'll have a lot in common with members
Join the 96 Club today. Call Ifeelit.

Not Gray

My hair isn't gray, it's white,
As white as the winter snow.
I now appear as an elderly
Even though I am still on the go.

Memory

I need you more then ever
To remember the good times I had.
I laughed a lot,
I talked a lot,
I even ran and walked a lot.
I made new friends,
I saw new places.
Memory, do not leave me.
Please stay forever.

Confusion

It's dark outside and I don't know
If it is morning or night.
There is no moon,
There is no sun,
My brain is confused and that's not right.
There are no stars in the sky,
Everything is quiet as can be.
Should I dress or stay in bed?
I'll just wait and see.

Why am I tired?
Could it be my age?
I can't accomplish anything and I am
    outraged.
I can easily sleep
All day and night,
I have to force myself to move and
That isn't right.
If I don't sign up for a program and make
    myself stay
I shall end up in my bed
Sleeping the rest of the day.

Daily Activities

My eldest son asked what I do all day.
He said it looks as if I have nothing to do.
I told him when I wake up:
I go into the shower
With a washcloth on my lap.
I must not forget to wash my ears,
They are under the shower cap

I wash my arms and legs, my face and nose,
Then I wash my ten little toes.
Now I'm clean and ready to face the day
    ahead.
Will it be one that I like or one that I dread?

I go into the kitchen,
Eat breakfast and take my meds,
I have to be sure that I am well fed.
I eat an orange and Quaker instant oatmeal,
I would say that's a pretty good deal

I go outside to get the paper to be read,
I have to see who is living and which of my
    friends are dead.

I outlived my friends whom I talked to
 every day.
That's a challenge for the future,
It won't be easy, I will say

I have to exercise so I go for a walk,
If I see a neighbor then I stop and talk.
Nobody wants to walk today,
They don't want the virus coming their way

I still have laundry, I still have meals or
As my oldest son says, that's no big deal.
I welcome company who will take me
 out to eat,
That will be a day that can't be beat.

How to Help the Elderly

Once a month: Walk with them,
Talk with them,
Take them for a ride.
They look forward to your visit
And they will not hide.

They may need help with papers
that need to be organized.
They may need an escort when buying
    groceries,
Are you surprised?

Do not forget the elderly,
Take them out to eat,
They have a good appetite that can't be beat.

Sleep

I fell into the arms of Morpheus,
I'm tired as can be,
I'm in the arms of Morpheus,
Morpheus will bring sweet dreams to me.

Memory

There are so many things to remember,
I have to recall them every day.
I hope that my memory will never go away.

When I go into the shower
I have to remember the knobs:
Left is hot and right is cold,
Left is on and right is off.

Please don't leave, memory,
I need you every day.

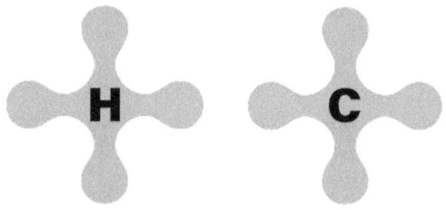

Raccoon

Mr. Raccoon, get out of my walls,
You are not wanted here.
Mr. Raccoon, get out of my house,
I hope you disappear.
You are an unwanted guest
Trying to live in my home.
If you don't immediately leave
I promise you will no longer roam,
And I keep my promises!

Itchit and Scratchit

Stay away from me, Itchit and Scratchit,
I do not like you!
The welcome mat in front of my home
Does not apply to you.

Chocolate

I think I'm addicted to chocolates,
Chocolate in any form:
Chocolate icing, chocolate cake,
Chocolate cookies that you bake,
Chocolate candy by the score.
Please pass the chocolates,
I think I'll have some more.

Fruit Fly

If I were a fruit fly and went to school
I would pay no attention to the golden rule.
On my report card I would get all A's
In multiplying and addition,
I'm great in that every day.

Lunch

I don't have to wonder
What to make for my lunch.
It will probably be pb&j,
It's easy to make
On two slices of bread.
It will carry me throughout the day.
At my age, I do things the easy way!

Think Before Getting Advice

I'm hesitant to ask anyone for advice,
I might end up with a bill which isn't
 very nice.
No one seem to help from the goodness of
 their heart,
They always think what's in it for me
Before they depart.

Trust

Having a friend is difficult,
It's hard as it can be,
You trust them with private information
Then just wait and see.
A calls me and talks about B,
B calls me and talks about A,
Then A calls B and they both talk about me.
The only person to trust is ME.

Memory

When I wake up in the morning
I have a paper and pen by my bed.
This is to record all happenings
For the day that lies ahead.
I have to remember what I see,
Writing on paper locks up
Words that might leave me.

Body

If you take care of your body
Your body will take care of you.
If you don't take care of your body
You'll become mixed up like a stew.
Your meals should consist of vegetables,
Cereals, salads, meat or fish.
If you take care of your body
You'll look like a pretty good dish.
DON'T FORGET TO WALK.

Blue

My eyes are hazel,
My hair is gray,
There are many colors going my way.
My favorite color is blue
Just like the sky above,
I have blue jeans and shirts
All of them I love.
I feel happy with clothes that are new,
I'm elated when I see you because
Then I don't feel blue.

Yousta

I used to be 5'1",
I'm now around 4'9".
I used to take walks by myself,
I now need an escort all of the time.
If this is what happens in the 90's
I hope I don't disappear.
I'll continue to think positive and
Look forward to another year.

Age 96

I am in a race with age,
So far I'm in the lead,
Age is starting to catch up with me
As you can plainly read.
A tooth fell out of my mouth,
My eyesight has decreased,
Hearing is not 100%
When you talk to me.

I intend to stick around and
Digest the news on paper and TV.
I shall win the race because
I'm not ready for age to take
The life out of me.

Going to the Bathroom Before Arrival of Ride to the Grocery Store

I have to go before they come,
They have to come after I go.
I made my list and I'm sure
For groceries I will have enough dough.

Love

Everyone seems to love me,
I daily receive their mail:
Mortgage companies, hearing aids,
 credit cards,
Bank loans and dates of a sale,
Places to help with depression and anxiety,
They are all interested in me.
My mail box is always full
From all who seem to love me.

Have To

I have to move forward
With what I've got,
I have my mind and body
And that's a lot.
I have to set in motion
My body and my mind
So they will advance forward
and not be left behind.

Chewing Gum

When you see the World Series
Be prepared and buy some gum,
Everyone chews like crazy
Especially if there is a home run.
If it's a no-hitter game
Like in 2022
Forget the gum because
Nothing happens when you chew.

Life Insurance

How many life insurance companies
Are there in the USA?
They all are calling me but
Hang up when I say 96.
96 always keeps them away.

Honesty

Someone is wearing my high school and
    college rings,
Also my sorority pin for real.
Some workers were not taught the
    8th Commandment
THOU SHALL NOT STEAL.

96 Click

My day started with a phone call saying
    "how are you today?"
When I said "fine," I thought I'd be
    on my way.
The caller said he had a plan to cover my
    needs when I'm dead.
I said, "That's great" because I have no life
    insurance for what lies ahead.
"Please tell me your age and I will see
    you soon."
When I said "96" I heard a sigh and a click,
He'll be seeing me in a blue moon!

Holiday

Do not get sick on a holiday,
The doctor won't answer the phone,
Do not get sick on a holiday,
You'll have to suffer all alone.
The pain seems unbearable in my toes
    and my right foot,
I must not get sick on a holiday,
I'll have to suffer all alone.

Growing Old

My stomach is getting fat,
My hair is getting thin,
My height is losing inches,
I can't seem to win.
I can think and I can talk,
When I take my daily walk at five
I have to be grateful
That I am still alive.

A Cluttered Room

Magazines and papers,
I've accumulated many,
I have to read them all
Even though they aren't worth a penny.

96

I'm sorry you don't qualify,
That's what I hear everyday.
My age sends life insurance callers
Not merrily on their way.

Deep Pockets

Please make pockets in my pants
To carry everything I need.
I need a comb for my hair
When the weather isn't fair,
I need a handkerchief for my nose
In case I have to sneeze,
I need money for a treat
If I go out to eat.
That's why taking gelt
Is always a big help.
So, if you please,
Make pockets when you manufacture
    my pants.

Age 96

I wake up with confusion in my brain,
I don't know if it's morning or night.
Why am I completely dressed
When outside there is no light?
My daughter calls me for dinner,
I'm shocked it's an evening meal.
Apparently I slept all day,
Now that's a very big deal.

I have to conquer age,
I must not let age take advantage of me,
I have to walk,
I have to talk,
I have to keep up with the news.
I have to activate my brain and
I can't continue singing the blues.

www.ingramcontent.com/pod-product-compliance
Lightning Source LLC
LaVergne TN
LVHW041714060526
838201LV00043B/725